TRICKS OF THE LIGHT

And Its Practical Uses
Judy Allen

Illustrated by Glenn Steward

Piccadilly Press, London

Typeset by Gilbert Composing Services
Printed and bound in Great Britain by
Garden City Press Ltd.
Letchworth, Herts.
for Piccadilly Press, London, 1985

Cover photograph by
David Parker/Science Photo Library Ltd.
The illustration on page 54 courtesy of Andrew Skilleter

Allen, Judy
    Tricks of the light: and its practical uses.
    1. Light—Juvenile literature
    I. Title   II. Steward, Glenn
    535   QC360

    ISBN 0-946826-75-7

Judy Allen lives in the Putney area of London and is an
experienced writer. Among her published works is the
adult fiction title, *December Flower*, published by
Duckworth in 1982 and several children's fiction titles.
Her adult non-fiction includes a number of guides for
Robert Nicholson. Judy also writes non-fiction for
children. Her books on new technology include *Chips,
Computers and Robots* (Puffin) 1983 and *Lasers and
Holograms* (Pepper Press) 1983.

CONTENTS

Introduction   7

1 LIGHT IN PERSPECTIVE
Light and the Electro-magnetic Spectrum   8

2 LIVE BEGINNINGS AND DEAD ENDS
Sources, Rays and Shadows   15

3 ON REFLECTION
Plane and Curved Reflecting Surfaces   20

4 BENDING THE RULES
Refraction   27

5 FROM PURE REFLECTIONS TO MIRAGES
Total Internal Reflection   32

6 HERE'S LOOKING AT YOU
Lenses and Eyes   35

7 PIGMENTS, PRISMS AND
POLARIZATION   40

8 USING LIGHT
Optical Instruments   45

9 LIGHT IN STEP
Lasers—Fibre Optics and Holograms   50

80125

10 STARLIGHT AND QUASARS
Astronomy and Astro-Physics   56

11 ARTFUL LIGHT
From Jewels to Paintings   59

Glossary   62

Index   64

INTRODUCTION

Visible light is essential to life. It is the original source of Light
energy. Not only does it warm the planet, it is also a form of
food. It makes plant life—and therefore the animal life
which feeds on it—possible, because green leaves combine
its energy with carbon dioxide from the air and with water
from their own cells to build the nourishment the plant
needs.

Light can be analyzed and understood. Natural light
behaves in different ways. It does not simply shine down
from above, it can reflect and refract and polarize. Light can
also be manipulated. It can be amplified, directed, or created
from another form of energy.

It can be coherent or incoherent. It can clarify or distort. It
can glow gently, as a baby's nightlight, or cleave solid metal
in two, as a laser. It can shine on this page so that you can
read it, carry your voice from one telephone to another along
fibre optic cables, or create 3-dimensional holographic
images that hang in the air like ghosts.

Without light there would be nothing. And it is this,
together with the fact that it can behave, or be used, in so
many different ways, that makes it such a uniquely
fascinating subject.

I LIGHT IN PERSPECTIVE

Light and the Electro-Magnetic Spectrum

Electro-magnetic radiations

Visible light is just one form of electro-magnetic radiation. Electro-magnetic radiations can travel through air or the vacuum of space at a speed of about 300,000 kilometres (or 186,000 miles, if you prefer) per second. Their natural source, so far as the earth is concerned, is the sun. However, because they have all been found to have their uses, science has devised ways of creating them all artificially.

Modern physics thinks of these radiations as individual particles of energy, called photons, which travel in a wave

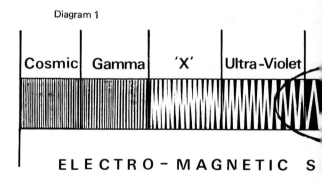

Diagram 1

Cosmic | Gamma | 'X' | Ultra-Violet

ELECTRO - MAGNETIC S

motion (actually, a transverse wave motion). Their wavelengths and frequencies can be measured. The wavelength is, literally, the length between each pair of waves. The frequency is, literally, the frequency with which they pass, worked out by counting the number of wavecrests passing per second.

The diagram shows the electro-magnetic spectrum—that is, all the radiations arranged in the order of their wavelengths. There is also a range of wavelengths within each section of the spectrum. Not all gamma rays, for example, vibrate on precisely the same wavelength, although they all vibrate within a specific range.

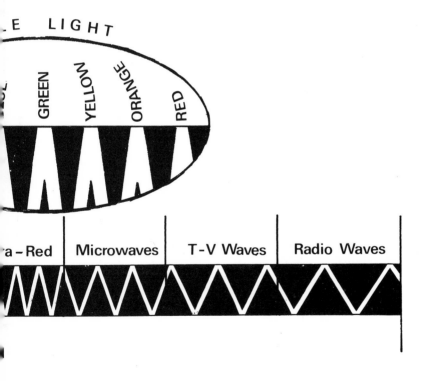

The radiations shown in the diagram are the ones we are aware of. It is possible that there are others, lying beyond each end of the spectrum, which we have not yet been able to detect.

Each group of radiations has different properties—and each can be used to produce different effects.

Cosmic rays

Cosmic rays have the shortest wavelengths and enormous energy. The origin of this intense energy, which is of great scientific interest, has not yet been defined. Some cosmic rays have their source in the sun but most come from beyond the solar system. The earth's atmosphere screens us from most of them, which is why they are best studied from satellites.

Gamma rays

Gamma rays—or γ rays—have the next shortest wavelengths and are quite dangerous. They, too, are high in energy. They can even pass through lead, unless it is extremely thick, and they damage living cells. They are given out by naturally radioactive material, radium and uranium for example, as well as by the sun. Plutonium, the radioactive material which is used in nuclear reactors, is manufactured artificially. Almost all natural gamma rays are screened by the earth's atmosphere.

X-rays

X-rays are next in line. (They were originally called X by the physicist who first discovered them because he didn't then understand them!) Artificially created X-rays are best known for their use in medicine. They pass straight through body tissue, but are absorbed by bones and teeth. So they can be directed through the body on to a photographic plate where the bones show up as black shadows—and breaks, cracks or displacements are clearly visible. Small, controlled doses are safe—prolonged exposure damages living tissue. Most natural X-rays are also screened by the earth's atmosphere.

Ultra-violet rays

Ultra-violet rays are not visible to us, although their effects are. Probably the most obvious of these is sun-tanning. Reasonable exposure is positively beneficial—it helps the body to produce vitamin D which is valuable for bones and teeth. Too much causes burning.

Visible light

Next to ultra-violet rays lies visible light. It is the wavelength of the light which determines the colour we see. The shortest most energetic wavelength produces the colour violet (next to the invisible ultra-violet) and the longest produces red (next to the largely invisible infra-red).

Because visible light is generally vibrating on all wavelengths at the same time, it is seen as white, or colourless. It is only when it is broken down into its separate wavelengths in some way—as it is in a rainbow—that we see the full range of colours. Reading from left to right along the diagram, from shorter wavelength to longer, these are violet, indigo, blue, green, yellow, orange, red. Of course, it isn't as cut and dried as that. For example, within the green part of the visible spectrum is contained a whole range of wavelengths from the bluey-greens through to the greeny-yellows.

Infra-red rays

Beyond visible red comes infra-red, generally invisible, although the eye can sometimes pick up a dim glow from it, and we can feel heat from it. Infra-red rays can go through body tissue to a certain extent, which is why they can be used medically to bring about changes in living tissue. They can also travel through haze and fog and, coupled with special optical equipment, can enable people to see, or to take photographs, in the dark without actually showing a light.

Radio waves

Microwaves are the shortest of the radio waves. They can be used for communications, in particular communica-

11

tions with satellites, because they can cut right through the ionosphere—the layers of gases in the upper atmosphere. They are used in radar, which works by bouncing them off an object and measuring the time they take to return, and the formation in which they return, to give an 'image' of its size, shape and its distance from the observer. They are also used to cook food, which they do by energising the molecules of which the food is composed so that they vibrate and give off heat, thus cooking the food from within. (It is almost as though the food in a microwave oven is made to rub its hands together, and so warm itself!)

The longer radio waves are used to transmit radio and television signals—from the high frequency (relatively short wavelengths) to the lower frequencies of longwave.

The transverse wave motion

Electro-magnetic waves are thought of as electric and magnetic vibrations which move at right angles to each other. See diagram 2. However, for the purposes of this book it isn't necessary to hold on to such a complicated image. But what is useful to know is that the waves move at right angles to their direction of travel. Again, see diagram 2. This is easiest to understand if you think of the waves of the sea. These waves move up and down on the vertical plane, but their direction of travel is along the horizontal plane. Diagram 3.

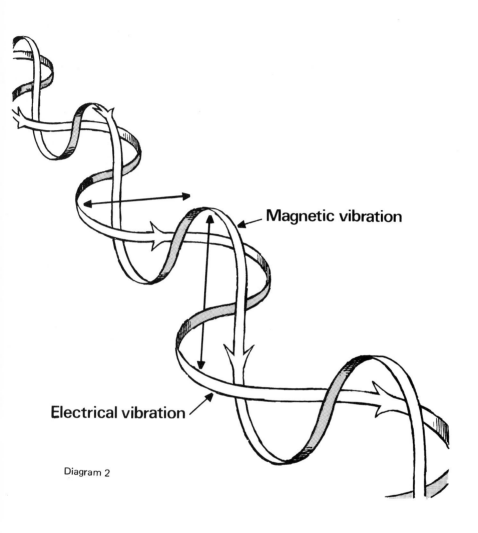

Magnetic vibration

Electrical vibration

Diagram 2

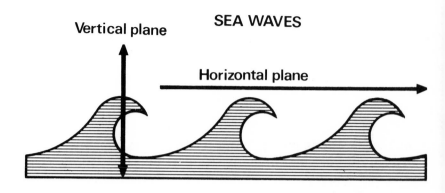

Diagram 3

2 LIVE BEGINNINGS AND DEAD ENDS
Sources, Rays and Shadow

Light is luminous energy, and it always has a source. The word 'luminous' means something which creates its own light—non-luminous objects simply reflect or pass on light which originated elsewhere.

How Light is Made

Light is created when a sudden input of energy causes the electrons orbiting an atom to jump to a higher energy orbit and then fall back.

If that doesn't explain it, here is a fuller explanation. An atom is the smallest particle of anything—so small that it cannot be divided without being destroyed. But it isn't solid. It is usually thought of as being made up of a nucleus or centre of protons (positive charges) and neutrons, surrounded by an orbiting cloud of electrons (negative charges). If something dramatic happens to the atom the electrons absorb energy and become excited. The kind of dramatic event the atom might experience is being given a shot of energy, or being split (nuclear fission) or being merged with another atom or atoms (nuclear fusion). The extra energy absorbed by the electrons sends them temporarily into a higher orbit around the atom, from which they eventually fall back exhausted. As each falls back again to a lower orbit it gives out a photon—the smallest particle of light energy.

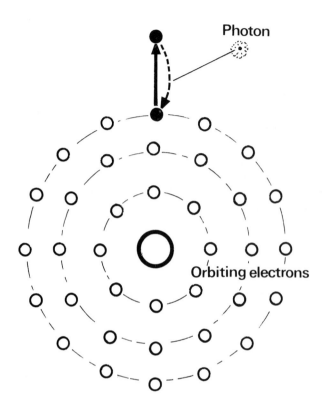

Sunlight and Moonlight

Our principal source of light, and of the rest of the electro-magnetic radiations (with the exception of the cosmic rays) is the sun. The sun, which is composed mainly of the two gases hydrogen and helium, has a temperature so intense that nuclear fusions take place within it all the time. To express a complex reaction very simply—what happens is that four atoms of hydrogen fuse together into one atom of helium. The reaction of the atoms and their electrons to this cataclysmic event is to produce radiant energy on all wavelengths, including visible light. Our sun, then, is a massive natural nuclear reactor, and so are the rest of the stars in the universe.

16

The moon though, however brightly it may shine, is a non-luminous object. It simply reflects the light of the sun. So do the planets, their moons, and the earth itself, as those who have travelled in space can testify.

Artificial light

Light can obviously be created artificially, but the principal is the same. In an electric light bulb, for example, electrical energy is fed in to the tungsten filament inside the bulb (which is itself filled with an inert gas, such as argon; if there was oxygen in there, the whole thing would burst into flames.) This energy excites the atoms making up the tungsten until their electrons are induced to give off light, and also heat.

Non-luminous objects

Any object that we can see—even if it does not appear actually to shine—is dealing with light in broadly the way that the moon does. It is non-luminous, in that it does not create light, but it gives off light, which strikes our eyes and gives us the sensation we know as sight. This page is an example. So is anything that you see around you when you look up—that is, unless it is a lamp or candle or something actually making light. (Physicists talk of the idea of an absolutely black body, which absorbs all radiations and neither reflects nor transmits any. But this is an idea, and not a reality).

Lantern fish and fireflies

Some living creatures make their own light. There are fish which live so deep in the oceans that no sunlight penetrates, and which carry colonies of bacteria on their bodies which produce light by a chemical reaction. Fireflies and glow-worms also carry their own lights. However, science has yet to work out exactly how these bacteria and insects produce their luminous patches, which seem to account for more energy than such small creatures could possibly generate. So it is wisest to ignore their impressive displays and concentrate on the kind of light about which something is known.

Rays and beams

Light usually travels in straight lines and the direction of its passage is known as a ray. Several rays make a beam. Although they travel in straight lines, the rays don't have to be parallel to each other. They can diverge—that is, spread outwards. Or they can converge—that is, follow a narrower and narrower path until they meet.

Shadows

If light meets a transparent obstruction—a glass window, perhaps—almost all of it passes through. If it meets something opaque, something which absorbs light—a book, perhaps, it is stopped dead. That is its end, it can go no further. Which is why you get shadows. If the source of the light is large—a strong lamp, say—then some of the rays will just graze by the edge of the opaque book and so the outline of the shadow will be fuzzy. A little light is getting through at the edges. But the centre of the shadow, where no light falls, will be black. The full shadow is known as the umbra. The partial shadow at the edge is the penumbra.

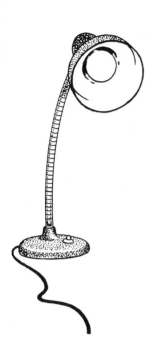

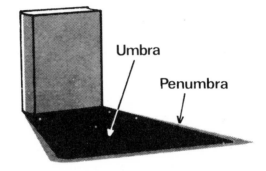

Umbra

Penumbra

3 ON REFLECTION

Plane and Curved Reflecting Surfaces

Light does not have a simple choice between going straight through something transparent and being brought up short by something opaque. It may meet something which reflects it.

Reflecting from a flat mirror

All kinds of things reflect light, but some of them do it in a rather complicated way. The simplest reflecting surface is a flat or plane mirror. A mirror reflects because it is made of highly polished glass, which is transparent, backed with a coating of silver (protected by a covering of paint) which is opaque. The light goes through the glass but bounces back from the silver.

Because light travels in straight lines, a ray which hits the mirror at right angles to its surface—diagram 4—will bounce straight back along the same line. This is known as the 'normal'. The incoming ray of light is known as the 'incident ray', and the ray of light that reflects back from the mirror is the 'reflected ray'. So if the ray hits the mirror at right angles, the reflected ray bounces back along the 'normal'.

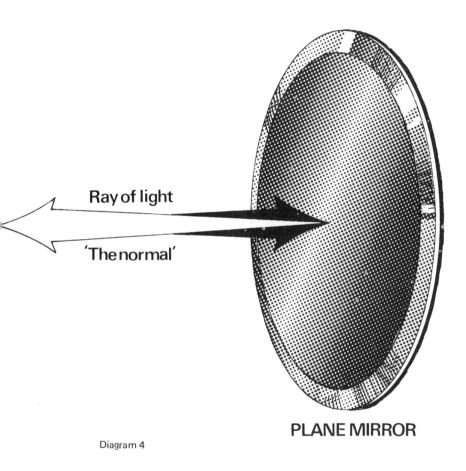

Ray of light

'The normal'

PLANE MIRROR

Diagram 4

The laws of reflection

However, not every ray hits a mirror head on. Some strike it at an angle, and there are two laws governing what happens next. One of these is that the incident ray, the normal and the reflected ray all lie in the same plane. In other words, they can always be drawn in diagram on a flat sheet of paper—you would not have to build a three-dimensional model to show their behaviour.

The other law is that the angle of incidence always equals the angle of reflection. That is, if you measure the angle between the incident ray and the normal, and the angle between the reflected ray and the normal, they will always be the same as each other. See diagram 5. The rest of the

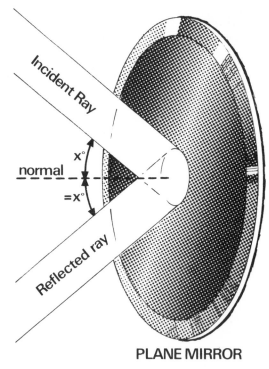

PLANE MIRROR

Diagram 5

electro-magnetic waves are governed by the same laws of reflection at plane surfaces as visible light.

The second law means that it is possible to redirect light, by means of mirrors, with absolute precision. As long as you know where the light is coming from, you can angle the mirror to send it where you want it to go. Think of a mirror at the entrance to a concealed drive, set up to show those using the drive whether or not the road is clear. Diagram 6.

Diagram 6

Mirror images

An image always seems to be as far behind the mirror as the object is in front. Move the object a little back from the mirror, and the image within the mirror will move back, too. The mirror-image is also laterally inverted. That is, the wrong way round, but not the wrong way up.

23

Reflecting at irregular surfaces

That's mirrors, and they give what are known as regular reflections. But most of the surfaces which reflect light—the moon, this page, your hand, the walls and so on are not highly polished, and they give irregular or diffuse reflections. The light seems to come off them in a rather slap-happy way. However, the laws of reflection are still in force. At any given point on the surface, the angle of incidence is equal to the angle of reflection. But because the surface is uneven (however smooth it may look to the eye) the incident rays strike it at many different angles, so sending the reflected rays off at as many different angles.

Kaleidoscopes

Fancy reflections can be created by the careful placing of mirrors. Two mirrors placed at right angles to each other will produce multiple reflections of an object placed between them—because it will reflect in each mirror, and the reflections themselves will re-reflect. This is how a kaleidoscope achieves its effects.

Curved mirrors

Curved mirrors produce different effects to flat or plane mirrors. A convex mirror, one which is curved outwards like the back of a spoon, is hit by rays coming from more directions than is a plane mirror. And because the angle of incidence equals the angle of reflection, it causes the reflected light rays to diverge outwards more than a plane mirror can, so giving a wider though smaller image. Convex mirrors are particularly useful as driving mirrors because they can reflect a wide area of the road behind in a scaled-down version, which makes it very easy to see what's going on.

A concave mirror, one which is curved inwards like the bowl of a spoon, causes the reflected light rays to converge, so producing a narrower but larger image. A concave mirror, then, is good for close detail—shaving mirrors, dentists' mirrors—because it reflects a small area in some detail.

The face in the spoon

If you look at yourself in the bowl of a spoon you see yourself upside down. But the images in shaving mirrors and dentists' mirrors are the right way up. Why?

Which way up you reflect in a concave mirror is determined by the mirror's focal length and where you are in relation to it. The focal length is the point at which the reflecting rays would be seen to cross, if you drew them as a diagram according to the laws of reflection, Diagram 7. If you are beyond the focal length you appear upside down. If you are within it, you appear the right way up. The more

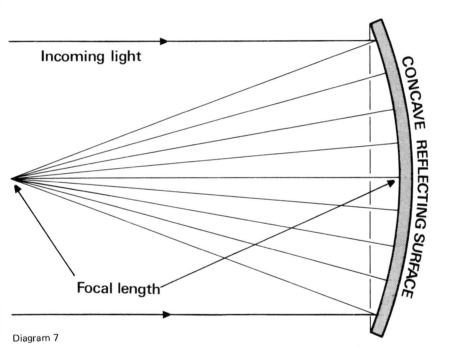

Diagram 7

curved a concave mirror is, the shorter its focal length. So a shaving mirror, which is only slightly curved, gives you a right-way-up image at any reasonable distance. (Though if you have good eyesight you can probably get far enough away from it to see yourself reflected upside down).

A spoon is so deeply curved that it has a very short focal length. To see yourself the right way up in a spoon you have to hold it so close you'll probably only be able to see the reflection of your eye—though it will be right way up. (As you move the spoon towards you there will come a disconcerting moment when you see two eyes, one above the other, one upside down and the other right way up. A little nearer, and they seem to merge!)

4 BENDING THE RULES

Refraction

Light does not travel at the same speed through all transparent mediums. It is at its top speed when travelling through a vacuum. It travels barely any slower through air. But water slows it down. And glass slows it down even more.

False depths

So when a light ray passes from one transparent medium to another, its speed changes, and this change of speed causes the ray to bend or, in other words, to refract. That is why water in a bowl or swimming pool always looks shallower than it actually is. And it is also why, if you put a long straight stick half in and half out of water, it will look as though it is bent.

The reason for this bending is that if the beam hits the water at an angle (and if you think about it, you see that light very rarely hits a surface head-on) some of the rays will hit the water before others. The ones which strike the water first will be slowed down first, so causing the light to bend. When the light leaves the water, again at an angle, the same thing happens in reverse. The rays first out of the water speed up first, and the rest of them catch up as and when they can. This causes the light to bend in the opposite direction.

To get an image of what happens, imagine a line of people, all walking in step, approaching a stream at an angle, wading through it, and coming out on the other side. Those first in to the water will be the first to be slowed down. The others, still going at the original speed, will gain on them, so bending the line. But the first in to the water will be the first out, and in speeding up before the rest, will cause the line to bend in the other direction. Diagram 8.

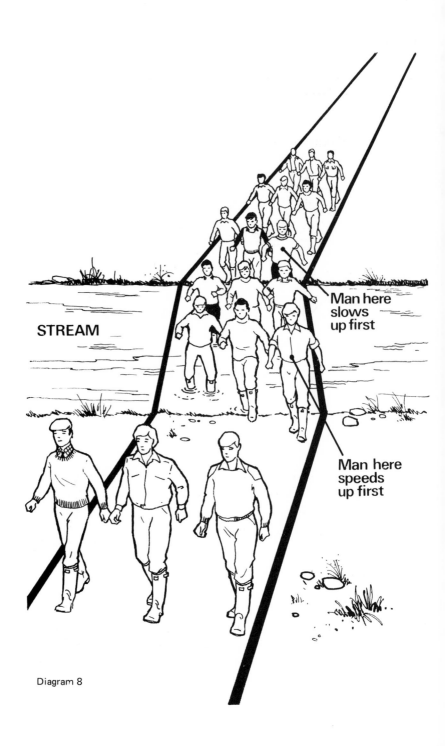

STREAM

Man here
slows
up first

Man here
speeds
up first

Diagram 8

So the light coming up from the bottom of a swimming pool will bend as it leaves the water and moves into the air. The eye assumes that the light is travelling in a straight line and so gets a false idea of the position of the bottom of the pool. See diagram 9.

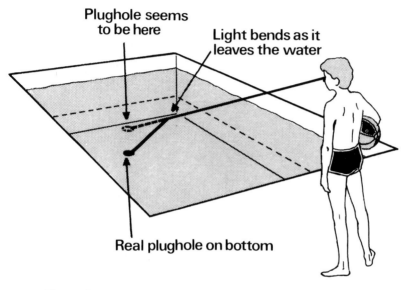

Plughole seems to be here

Light bends as it leaves the water

Real plughole on bottom

Diagram 9

There is also a weak, reflected ray—see diagram 10 next page. So quite a lot is going on. The incoming ray strikes the water and is refracted. A strong refracted ray goes to the bottom of the pool and a weak reflected ray is given off. The bottom of the pool reflects the light back up, at the surface it is refracted, and again gives off a strong refracted ray and a weak reflected ray.

The critical angle

Not all light rays travelling from water to air actually make it out into the air. It depends on the angle at which they approach. If the angle is what is known as 'critical' they will not come clear of the water but will travel along its surface.

29

This means that all you will see will be a lot of sparkling on the surface of the water—you won't see the bottom of the pool at all.

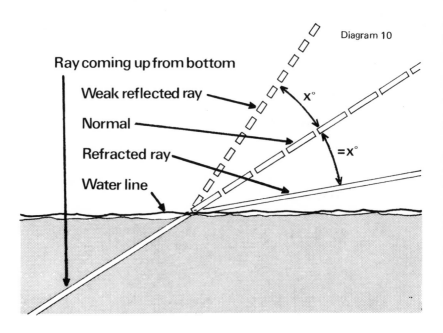

Diagram 10

Ray coming up from bottom

Weak reflected ray

x°

Normal

=x°

Refracted ray

Water line

The laws of refraction

There are two laws governing refraction. Just as in reflection there is an incident ray, a reflected ray and a 'normal'—so in refraction there is an incident ray, a refracted ray and a 'normal'. And the first law states that the light bends towards the normal when the incident ray enters a denser medium at an angle (when it goes from air into the water, for example). And that it bends away from the normal when the incident ray enters a less dense medium at an angle (when it goes from water to air, for example). The second law says that the incident ray, the refracted ray and the 'normal' all lie in the same plane, and so can all be drawn in diagram —see diagram 10 for proof!

Although air and water have been used as examples, the laws of refraction apply whatever transparent medium the light is going into or out of, as long as one is denser than the other.

30

The refractive index

It is possible to calculate the exact angle of refraction that will occur if light passes, at a known angle, from air (or, strictly, a vacuum) into another transparent medium. This is known as the 'refractive index' and tables have been compiled stating how the light will behave when passing through, for example, specific types of glass. This information is invaluable when preparing lenses, and prisms, see Chapters 6 and 7.

Bending the starlight

Light can be refracted on a large scale, as well. Because the atmosphere surrounding the earth is denser than the vacuum of space, the rays of the sun are subject to atmospheric refraction. This means that you can still see an image of the sun for a short while after it has actually set below the horizon. It also means that astonomical observers don't actually see the stars in their true positions (something which astronomers have to take into account in observations and calculations).

Bending the radio waves

The rest of the electro-magnetic radiations are subject to the same laws—which is why it is possible for radio waves to travel around the earth. Since they, like light waves and the rest, travel in straight lines, they ought simply to shoot off into space and disappear. As it is, they encounter a layer of electrical particles in the upper atmosphere which, because it is denser than the atmosphere below, causes refraction, which bends the waves and allows them to continue around the earth.

5 FROM PURE REFLECTIONS TO MIRAGES

Total Internal Reflection

When light shines from a less dense medium into a denser one, from air into glass or water, the result is almost always a strong refracted ray, going into the glass at an angle and a weak reflected ray coming out of it—at an angle from the normal equal to the incident ray, as dictated by the laws of reflection. See diagram 11.

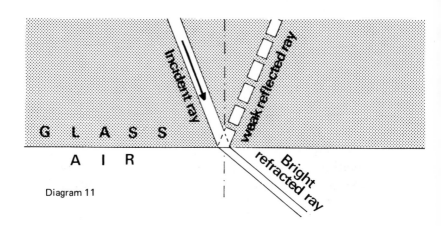

Diagram 11

However, if the light is travelling from a denser medium to a rarer one, from glass or water into air, there is a different result. As the angle of incidence is increased so the angle of refraction increases—still producing a strong refracted ray and a weak reflected ray—until, at what is known as a 'critical angle of incidence', the refracted ray just skims along the boundary between the two mediums.

If the angle is increased still more, the light is not refracted at all—and the dim reflected ray all at once becomes bright. This is the effect known as 'total internal reflection of light'. See diagram 12.

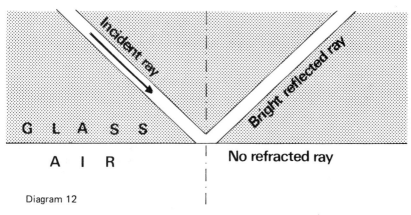

Diagram 12

Because the light is totally internally reflected, the ray that comes out is pure. It is not distorted and it is not divided into a refracted ray and a weak reflected ray. It is all pure reflection, so it can carry with it a very clear image.

Prisms

The effect is used in the prisms which takes the place of mirrors in good quality periscopes (and the prisms in prism binoculars). The trouble with an ordinary plane mirror is that there are often multiple reflections going on inside the glass which result in multiple images on its surface. This is only noticeable if the mirror and its reflections are examined very closely, so ordinarily it doesn't matter. But when it comes to precision optical instruments, it does matter. And a prism which is capable of total internal reflection of light gives a single, perfect image.

Optical fibres

The effect also makes optical fibres possible. These are extremely fine fibres of spun glass with a very high refractive index. (The higher the refractive index the lower the critical angle. So a high refractive index increases the probability of total internal reflection).

The total internal reflection effect means that light can be trapped inside these fibres, and sent along them, reflecting

33

off the sides as it goes, until allowed out at the end. The fibres are coated with glass of a lower refractive index which prevents the light from beaming out at the sides and dispersing its energy. See diagram 13.

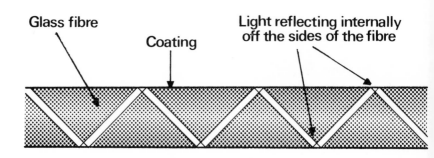

Diagram 13

Because the light that comes out at the end of the fibres is very clear and pure, it can bounce back a very true image of what it finds at one end to the other end. This means that a group of optical fibres can be used very effectively to examine tricky corners—such as the inner workings of delicate machinery, people and animals.

If the original light source is a laser, optical fibres can be used for digital communications, see Chapter 9.

Mirages

Total internal reflection can also account for mirages. Probably most people have seen, on a hot day, a mirage of water on the road. This happens because the air just above the hot tarmac is warmer than the rest of the air. Warm air has a smaller refractive index than cool air (though the difference is only slight) and when the light travels from the cooler air to the warm lower air at a critical angle, total internal reflection takes place and an image of the bright sky appears on the road—where it looks just like a pool of shimmering water.

6 HERE'S LOOKING AT YOU

Lenses and Eyes

An optical lens is a specially shaped piece of transparent material—often glass—which can manipulate the light rays that pass through it. Basically, the surface of a lens is either convex or concave. (Although to achieve special effects, two or more lenses may be used at once. And even a single lens may be convex on both sides, concave on both sides, or convex on one side and concave on the other.)

Convex and concave lenses

A convex, converging or positive lens causes the light rays to converge—and so magnifies the image. A concave, diverging or negative lens causes the light rays to diverge, and so gives a smaller image.

The light passing through a convex lens is refracted, or bent, until it converges at a point known as the principal focus, see Diagram 14. This is a real focus, because an actual image is formed there, one that could be shown on a screen.

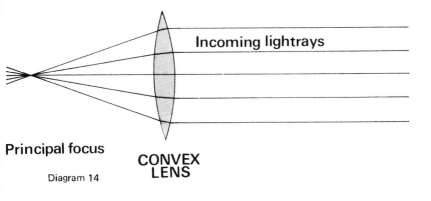

Incoming lightrays

Principal focus

CONVEX LENS

Diagram 14

35

A concave lens has a principal focus which is known as 'virtual' and is behind the lens. It is the point from which the refracted beam of light seems to diverge, but there is no actual image there that could be shown on a screen. See diagram 15.

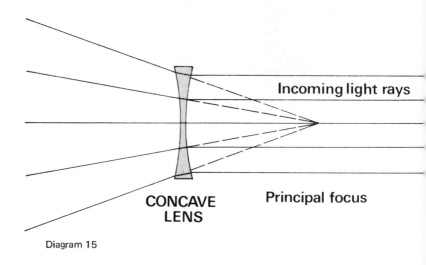

Incoming light rays

Principal focus

CONCAVE LENS

Diagram 15

Focal Length

The distance from the optical centre of the lens to the principal focus is the focal length. This length is determined by the size and shape of the lens. The shorter the focal length the more powerful the lens because the more it causes the light rays to converge or diverge.

The lens of the eye

The eye itself has a lens, see diagram 16. It is behind the black-looking pupil in the centre. The ciliary muscles can change the shape, and so the focal length of the lens. Also, the iris, the coloured part of the eye, can contract or expand to reveal more or less of the lens through its central hole or pupil, according to the amount of light available. (The brighter, the smaller.)

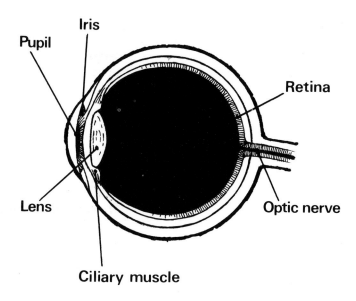

Diagram 16

The lenses of eyes with perfect vision cause the incoming light rays to converge on a point of the retina, at the back of the eye, where chemicals react to them and send electrical signals along the optic nerve to the brain.

Because of the way the rays converge—the ray coming from the highest part of the image striking the lowest part of the retina and the ray from the lowest part of the image striking the highest part of the retina—Diagram 17—the image at the back of the eye is upside down. But, and no one

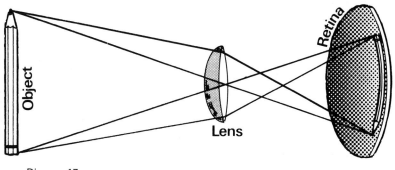

Diagram 17

yet knows quite how this happens, the brain conveniently turns the image the right way up again.

Short-sighted eyes

A short sighted eye is actually too long which causes the rays of light to converge in front of the retina which is why short sighted people try to get their eyes as near as possible to anything they are reading in order to send the image far enough back. Concave lenses in a pair of spectacles will cause the light to diverge just before it strikes the lenses of the eyes. The lenses of the eyes are then dealing with rays coming in from a wider angle, so that when they cause them to converge, they meet where they should, on the retina. Diagram 18.

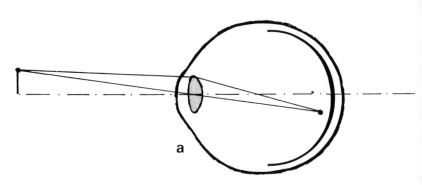

a

Lengthened eye (Short sight)

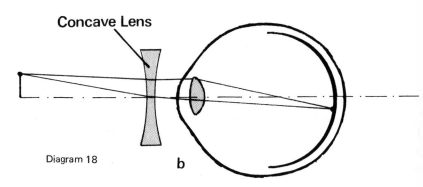

Concave Lens

Diagram 18

b

Long-sighted eyes

A long sighted eye is actually too short causing the light rays to converge behind the retina—which is why long sighted people tend to pull back from whatever they are reading. Spectacles with convex lenses begin the job of converging the rays, which the lenses of the eyes can then successfully complete. Diagram 19.

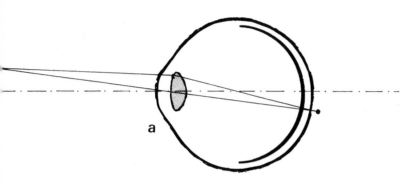

Shortened eye (Long sight)

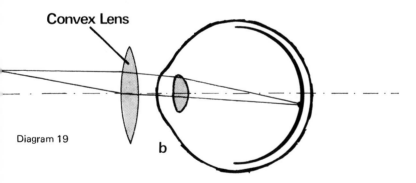

Convex Lens

Diagram 19

Optical instruments

Lenses are used in cameras, which work much as the eye does, and in projectors. They also form the most important parts of binoculars, telescopes and microscopes, which are used to magnify images to greater or lesser extent.

7 PIGMENTS, PRISMS AND POLARIZATIO

As was seen in Chapter One, if light is vibrating on all its possible wavelengths and frequencies at the same time, it appears to be white.

In the same way, an object which is seen as white is one which is reflecting back all the different wavelengths. That is why white clothes are considered suitable for summertime, and appropriate for activities like tennis and cricket. Light is also heat, and in reflecting it back white clothes keep the wearer cooler.

Something which is seen as black, on the other hand, is absorbing all the rays and reflecting back almost none of them—so, by giving off virtually no light, it imitates darkness and is black. That is why people tend to feel warmer in black clothes.

Pigment colour

The colour you see when you look at an object is known as pigment colour. It is the colour which is reflected, while all other colours are being absorbed. So in a curious way when you say an object is blue, what you are really saying is that blue is the one wavelength of light that the object is rejecting; the colour it turns away, or reflects, is the colour it is said to be. The term 'pigment' is also used for the coloured substances used in making artists' coloured paints (and, indeed, decorators' paints).

Transmitted colour

The colour of coloured glass—in stained glass windows, green bottles and the like—is not pigment colour but transmitted colour, because these glasses have the appearance of being the colour they transmit, or allow to pass through them.

The light-bending prism

A prism, see diagram 20, which can be used to create total internal reflection and so form a superior reflecting medium, can also be used to separate white light into the frequencies (or wavelengths) which constitute it, and so make visible its separate colours.

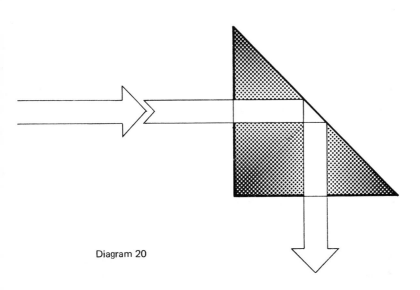

Diagram 20

The prism can separate the light into colours because its refractive index is different for each colour. See diagram 21. Therefore, as the white, or mixed, light passes through the prism, each colour is refracted at a slightly different angle, and they come out separately, in the order we know from seeing rainbows—red, orange, yellow, green, blue, indigo, violet. This coloured band, within the electro-magnetic spectrum, is also called a spectrum. (It also follows that if coloured lights are mixed, the result is white light.)

41

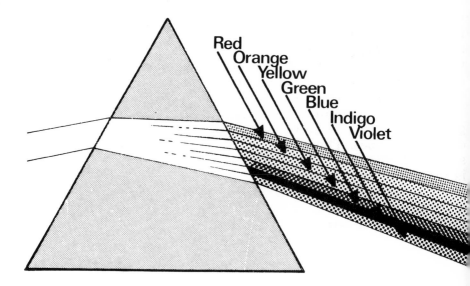

Diagram 21

The rainbow

A rainbow is formed because individual drops of water, falling through the air as rain (or still suspended in the air just after it) act as natural prisms and refract the sunlight down into its separate component colours. Sometimes, further internal reflection takes place and you get a secondary rainbow, below the primary one, in which the colours are reversed.

Polarizing crystals

Prisms disperse light into its component colours, but certain crystals, especially tourmaline and quartz, do something different to light—they polarize it. Natural light waves, in common with all electro-magnetic waves, generally vibrate in all possible directions, at right angles to the direction of the wave. (See diagram on transverse wave motion on page 13). When light is polarized, all its vibrations go in the same direction.

42

Plane polarization

There are various kinds of polarization, but the simplest to understand is plane polarization. This can be caused naturally when light rays encounter certain crystals, such as tourmaline, whose atomic structure is such that it restricts the vibrations by transmitting, or passing on, only the waves which are vibrating in a single direction, in line with its internal structure.

To get an image of what happens—think of a random group of transverse vibrations, and imagine they are all different shapes. Then think of a sieve with holes of one shape. (Diagram 22). The shapes are the light, and the sieve is the structure of the crystal. You can see that when the shapes meet the sieve, only certain ones will get through. Vibrations going in any other directions, shown here as different shapes, are simply blocked.

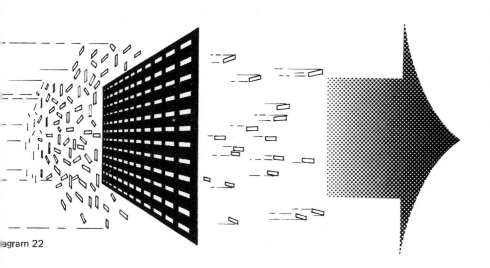

Diagram 22

43

Experiments with these crystals have led to the ability to produce the polarizing effect artificially and at will. Reflected glare can be a nuisance, even a hazard, and polarization reduces it. Polaroid sunglasses, as an example, are made of crystalline material with similar properties and structure to tourmaline—and this effectively cuts down the amount of light they will allow to pass through them.

8 USING LIGHT

Optical Instruments

The healthy eye can see and examine objects which vary enormously in size—from planets to insects. But spectacles, magnifying glasses, microscopes and telescopes open up whole worlds we would otherwise know nothing about.

When the behaviour of light begins to be understood, it is possible to create optical instruments which can manipulate it in useful ways. The camera uses light to record a scene; other optical instruments bend it to magnify images.

Cameras

The camera—for all its seeming complexity—is basically a very simple instrument. It is really only a lightproof box through which is passed a film, containing light sensitive chemicals. It has a shutter, which opens and closes rather as an eyelid does, to expose the film to light for the right amount of time. In many cameras, shutter speeds can be varied to achieve different effects. While the shutter is open, the light waves reflecting from any object at which the camera is pointing will enter, strike the film and form a negative image there (which becomes positive when the film is printed). There is also a lens, through which the incoming light is focused—and if the lens is adjustable the focus can be sharpened by moving it away from or towards the film— usually by turning a ring which moves the lens within the camera. In many cameras, the aperture of the lens can also be adjusted, to control the amount of light admitted.

Even the most sophisticated cameras are a version of that basic model, and the only aim of all their gadgets and microprocessor abilities is to control the amount and duration of light admitted to the film, thereby controlling the appearance and quality of the final print or transparency.

Magnifying glasses

To examine an object in detail, we have to bring it as close to the eye as possible. The closer we look, the larger the object seems to be—but also, the closer we look the more blurred the object becomes. The magnifying glass overcomes this difficulty. It uses a convex lens which causes the light rays passing through it to converge before they reach the lens of the eye (which will itself cause them to converge on the retina). The convex lens sends the light rays from the object that is being viewed into the eye at a wider angle than if the eye looks at the object unaided. This means that the image received by the retina is larger than usual, and so the object appears larger than it is. The more convex the lens the more it magnifies, but the shorter its focal length. In other words, the more convex it is, the closer you have to be to the object and the more the image is distorted.

Microscopes

A microscope uses more than one convex lens—to increase the size of the image and to reduce distortion. The first lens magnifies the image of the object. The second lens, otherwise known as the eyepiece, magnifies the magnified image, and so on.

Telescopes

The human eye admits too little light to make much sense of distant stars, so telescopes are designed to take in as much light as possible and to focus it down into an image on the retina. The refractor telescope works by means of convex lenses—in a smaller way, though on a larger scale, as magnifying glasses and microscopes. The strength of a refractor, or lens, telescope is limited by the size of the lenses it can support.

The reflector telescope works by using a vast concave mirror to gather in the light, and it can be much larger because the mirror is at the back of the structure and can be supported. The light rays coming from the stars strike the mirror, are reflected from it, and then strike a small plane mirror which reflects a real image. The real image is then

magnified by lenses in the eyepiece of the telescope.

In all these optical instruments, the magnifying power depends not only upon the size and convexity of the lenses but also on the skill of the lens maker.

Radio telescopes

Radio telescopes, of course, are quite different. They don't pick up light waves but the slower radio waves, which come in so feebly that a huge moveable dish has to be used to catch them, and the telescope and its ancillary equipment must be capable of focusing and then amplifying all that it has caught.

9 LIGHT IN STEP

Lasers, Fibre Optics and Holograms

The fact that light is energy, and that it can be organised in such a way that it works for us, becomes clear when you consider the laser and the technological advances it has made possible. Lasers and holograms are described in detail in a book of that name, and fibre optics in a book called **Electronic Wizardry** (see back cover), but here is a brief look at these ordered uses of light.

Why the laser lases

A laser gives off a beam of light. Yet it is about as different from a torch beam as a battering ram is from a pile of sawdust.

All that a torch can do is use the power of its batteries to stimulate the atoms of the filament in the bulb until their electrons jump to a higher excited state. In a very short time they will, as a rule, drop back to their normal state, giving off as light the excess energy. This light is created in limited quantities, on most of the lower wavelengths and frequencies at once (which is why the beam is yellowish white) and allowed to diverge outwards in a widening beam until it disperses.

In a laser, on the other hand, not only are the orbiting electrons excited into producing light, but also the light energy coming from one electron is capable of causing another electron to jump a level, drop back and give off light energy and so on. This means that the light energy builds up and up.

The laser gets its name from this ability—the name is an acronym (being made up of the initial letters of the words which describe the technique). It stands for Light

Amplification by Stimulated Emission of Radiation. And if you think that through you will see that it is just that!

But the laser does more than amplify the light it creates; it also creates the light at a specifically selected wavelength and frequency. Therefore, as all the waves are in step, they reinforce each other (whereas with ordinary chaotic light a trough and a peak may arrive together and cancel each other out.) Because it is all on one wavelength and frequency (or as nearly so as possible) laser light is said to be 'in phase' or 'coherent'.

What is more, the laser tube is so long and narrow that the light comes out in a beam which is not only intensely bright and powerful, but which travels in a straight narrow beam which hardly diverges outwards at all.

The lasing medium

The collection of atoms the laser works with is known as the lasing medium or the active medium. It can take the form of a gas, a liquid or a solid (usually a synthetic crystal).

The source of energy

The laser also needs a means of pumping energy into the lasing medium. The first ruby laser, which was a crystalline rod of synthetic ruby into which a small quantity of the metal chromium had been introduced, used a powerful xenon flash-lamp. It is also possible to use electrical energy, or to use one laser as the energy source for another.

The structure

The central part of the laser is the long resonator tube—in which all the activity takes place. At each end there is a mirror which reflects back the newly created photons of light. The photons race to and fro, bouncing off the mirrors, colliding with the atoms of the lasing medium and stimulating them into producing more photons on the same wavelength. Because the mirror at the business end of the laser is only partly silvered, the beam is allowed to escape. The whole process, from the switching on of the power to the emission of the beam, is so fast it appears to be instantaneous.

The laser's uses

Laser light can be used industrially, for cutting, boring and welding. It can be used medically for similar purposes—cutting human tissue, welding a detached retina back into place, and even removing some tattoos and skin cancers. Because the beam is so straight it can be used as a surveyor's ruler, to measure and also to align things (two ends of a new bridge, for example). Because the speed of light is known it can be used to measure distance. A laser beam bounced off a mirror on the moon, set up there by the first astronauts, can be used to check the precise distance of the moon from the earth at any given time. It can be a defensive weapon, shooting down missiles (although it is less useful for attack because it is not easily portable). It can also stimulate the atoms in certain gases and solids to behave in particular ways, which means it is being used to create nuclear fission, is being used in research into nuclear fusion, and is invaluable for chemical analysis.

Fibre optics

Laser light can also be used to carry digital signals along optical fibres. Digital signals can as easily take the form of pulses of light as of electrical pulses, and now that reliable methods have been developed of making strong, fine, supple fibres of ultra-pure glass (a minute impurity in the glass could scatter the light or pull it up short) fibre optic links have become the most efficient communications links available.

Each hair-fine fibre consists of a transparent glass core and a cladding, or covering, of glass with a lower refractive index, so that the light does not come out at the sides. The light suffers total internal reflection and so bounces down the fine central core in a very pure state. Optical fibres are light in weight, flexible, strong, relatively cheap to make, unaffected by electro-magnetic interference, and have an immense carrying capacity. If damaged they don't give an electric shock, and the light from any broken ends does not have enough energy to cause a fire or spark off an explosion.

They can form most kinds of communications links, connecting the separate parts of a computerised systems or carrying telephone, radio and television signals. And they can be used to carry back images from tight corners. They are so fine they can easily be passed down the throats of sick people or animals, or pushed into tight corners in delicate machinery.

Holograms

A hologram is a kind of ghost-like three-dimensional photograph, so effective you believe your hands will be able to feel the contours of the object shown. Yet touch a hologram and all you will find is a flat, shiny surface.

All images depend on light, but holography depends on coherent laser light. The technique is similar to a conventional photographic technique. But while a photographic negative makes sense to the eye, a hologram does not—that is, not until it is lit by a bright light which strikes it at the correct angle.

Making a hologram

The diagram on the next page gives an idea of how the basic split-beam technique works.

The coherent light of a laser beam (1) is directed by a mirror (2) into a device known as a beam-splitter (3) which does just that – splits the beam in two. One of these is known as the reference beam (4) which is directed by another steering mirror (5) through an expanding lens (6). This lens spreads the light on to a holographic plate at a precise angle (7). Simultaneously the other beam, known as the object beam (8) is directed by a steering mirror (9) through an expanding lens (10). This lens spreads the light all over the subject (11) which reflects it.

The light waves reflected from the subject meet the light waves from the reference beam (12) on the surface of the plate, which is coated with minute light-sensitive crystals. Because both light sources originated in the same laser they are of exactly the same wavelength. They are therefore able to coincide and create what is known as an interference wavefront. This interference wavefront records the shape and depth of the subject on the holographic plate.

The uses of holography

Holographic art is becoming more and more popular but the technique does have serious uses too. Some modern computers have optical memories made up of tiny holograms which encode information in patterns of light and dark dots. A hologram of a micro-organism has the effect of making something minute and fast-moving hold still while it is examined (while not flattening it or distorting it as an ordinary photograph would). Holograms of priceless items can be sent out on travelling exhibitions while the originals stay safely home in a vault. A hologram on a credit card makes forgery nearly impossible. And there are specialised computers which can create holographic models of buildings, machinery or tools, which can then be adapted and redesigned far more rapidly than could a physical model.

Other possibilities

There are possibilities, too, of quite different holograms. At the moment, lasers work with visible light, but as the whole **electro-magnetic spectrum is subject to the same laws there** is, in theory, no reason why a laser should not amplify other wavelengths and frequencies. Research into the possibilities of x-ray lasers is under way, and this could lead to x-ray holography—and to very detailed views of living cells and their problems.

Holographic interferometry—or how to spot stress

Holographic interferometry is a useful spin-off. The smallest vibration of an object when a hologram is being made causes the light waves to bounce back at unexpected angles which creates curious visual effects, known as an interference fringe, on the finished hologram. This means that the technique can show if something which should not be moving or vibrating, in fact is. This has revolutionised strain analysis on aircraft and engine components—in which even minute vibrations at high speed could be disastrous.

IO STARLIGHT AND QUASARS

Astronomy and Astro-Physics

Astronomy relies on the picking up and analysing of the electro-magnetic radiations given off by the various different kinds of star and matter that make up the universe. Early astronomy was dependent on visible light—collected and magnified by telescopes. More recently, radio telescopes have made it possible to collect radiations that fall into other parts of the electro-magnetic spectrum. And more recently still, observatories have been sent into orbit on board satellites, where they can pick up light and other electro-magnetic wavelengths, beyond the distorting interference of the earth's atmosphere.

Time and Space

An astronomer studying anything in the universe outside our solar system is actually looking back in time—and so is anyone who looks up at the night sky. Even the nearest stars are so far away that their distance is measured in light years—the length of time it has taken the light to reach us at its known speed of 186,000 miles per second. A light year equals 9.5 million million kilometres. The nearest star, apart from the sun, is four and a half light years away, but galaxies have recently been detected which are well over a million million light years away.

Wavelengths and Movements

Astro-photography can produce surprisingly clear results, even from the 'wrong' side of the earth's atmosphere, if the camera shutter is left open for long enough. When allied to a spectroscope, astro-photography can break down the spectrum given off by a star into its separate wave-

56

lengths, thereby giving an enormous amount of information about its behaviour and structure. All matter is made up of ninety-two elements, each of which (or each group of which) produces a different and recognisable effect in the spectroscope, which means that spectroscopy can show what any given light source is made of. It also makes it possible to study the so-called 'Doppler effect'. This is the apparent change in wavelength of radiations given off by bodies that are approaching or receding. Light approaching seems bluer, light receding shifts towards the red area of the spectrum. It is the 'red shift' of the distant galaxies that supports the idea that they are all moving away from us and each other. (Although the earth is no longer thought of as the centre of the universe, we can only make observations from where we are. So descriptions of what has been discovered sometimes seem to imply that the earth is central).

Quasars and other mysteries

Despite all the equipment and research, there are still mysteries, and substantial ones, too. Although the majority of astronomers support the Big Bang Theory, which says that all matter in the universe was once concentrated into a single lump which exploded, sending bits and pieces in all directions, and that the universe has continued to expand outwards ever since, no one knows for certain that this was so. And although attempts are frequently made to work out the age of the universe, they are really only educated guesses. And no one has yet been able to explain the intensely powerful quasars—quasi-stars, which are the reddest light sources in the universe and therefore presumably receding at great speed. In fact, one quasar seems to produce more energy than an entire galaxy, and to send it across the estimated ten million million miles that separates it from earth and her astronomers.

For a time it was suggested that quasars might actually be much nearer than calculations had suggested, that perhaps light behaves differently in deep space and the red shift of the quasars is misleading. However, recent discoveries of new galaxies at the edge of the universe which are close (relatively speaking!) to quasars, seems to confirm that they really are an exceedingly long way away, and that therefore their power in relation to their size is quite extraordinary. This leaves astronomy not only with a mystery but with the interesting problem of explaining something which contradicts all the known laws of physics!

11 ARTFUL LIGHT

From Jewels to Paintings

Artists, and those who work with glass and precious stones whose art is considered to be a craft, often use light for special effects. Sometimes the light is manipulated quite deliberately, as it is when holograms are made. Sometimes it is possible for the effects to be achieved by trial and error, so that the rules governing the behaviour of the light are not necessarily understood.

Stained glass

Glass obviously makes the most of light, even if the glass in question is only a simple drinking tumbler. But some of the most spectactular effects are created by so-called 'antique glass', which is still made today. This is the glass that was first used in the stained glass windows of medieval churches. The colours in stained glass are not pigment colour but transmitted colour (see page 40) because each piece appears to be the colour which it transmits, or allows to pass through it. So when the sun from outside a church strikes a piece of blue stained glass, only that light which is vibrating on the blue wavelength is allowed to pass through, making the glass glow, and sometimes falling to the floor of the church in a splash of colour.

Bubbles and faults

Another reason for the great beauty of medieval glass, and its modern equivalent, is the fact that it is handblown. It is blown into a long bubble, the ends are cut off to make a cylinder, and then the cylinder is split along its length and flattened into a sheet. And, because it is handblown it is uneven in thickness and even has the odd bubble actually in it. This unevenness refracts and reflects the light far more interestingly that a perfect sheet of glass ever could.

The cut glass angle

Cut glass also plays with light to add to its appeal. This glass, usually uncoloured, is cut into facets—or tiny angled surfaces—which receive the light and reflect it back at all kinds of angles, with sparkling results.

Diamonds are for dazzling

Anyone who has ever seen a rough or uncut diamond will know that it doesn't look up to much. But a cut diamond is beautiful and seems literally to blaze with light. This is because its facets have been deliberately angled so that, as well as causing refraction and reflection, they can subject the incoming light rays to total internal reflection, which means they give out pure, bright reflected rays.

The picture of light

Paintings obviously rely wholly on the effects of light and colour. But many painters have been concerned to depict light itself—not only light as it reflects from subjects, but light as a subject in itself. J.M.W. Turner is probably the most famous of those to have made the attempt.

Lasers and sunsets

The most wholly modern of the artistic uses of light are lasers and holograms, the construction and use of which is not so much an art or a craft as a feat of engineering and physics. And very effective the results are, too. But light, which is so much older than humanity, can create spectacular effects just by being there—with no interference from either art or science. There have been rainbows and sunsets, and mirages and eclipses, and the aurora borealis or northern lights since the beginning. And it is still true that most effects we can produce, by whatever means, are only dim imitations or small-scale variations on what has always been there.

GLOSSARY

Here is a quick check-list of some of the possibly unfamiliar terms used in this book.

ARGON. An inert gas (one which doesn't react chemically) often used in fluorescent lighting tubes and light bulbs.

ASTRO-PHYSICS. Research into the physical and chemical make-up of the stars and planets.

ATOM. The smallest particle of anything, which cannot be split without being destroyed.

CONCAVE. Being curved like the inside of a circle.

CONVEX. Being curved like the outside of a circle.

DIGITAL. A digital current or signal takes the form of pulses, unlike an analogue current or signal which is continuous.

ELECTRO-MAGNETIC RADIATIONS. Electric and magnetic fields which vibrate at right angles to each other. They range from radio waves to gamma or γ rays, and include visible light.

ELECTRO-MAGNETIC SPECTRUM. The complete range of known electro-magnetic vibrations.

ELECTRON. A negatively charged particle found in all atoms.

FACET. One side of an object with many sides—especially used to refer to cut gems.

FOCAL LENGTH. The distance between the centre of a lens or mirror and the focal point.

FOCAL POINT. The point at which a lens or mirror focuses.

FREQUENCY. When referring to radio or other electro-magnetic radiations—the time taken for succeeding wave crests to pass a given point.

LENS. Specially shaped device, often of glass, which causes light rays to converge or diverge.

LUMINOUS. Used of a source which creates light, as opposed to one which only reflects it.

NEUTRONS. Contained in the centre of all atoms (except hydrogen) and carrying no electrical charge.

NUCLEAR FISSION. Splitting an atom or atoms.

NUCLEAR FUSION. Joining, or fusing, two or more atoms together.

OPAQUE. Anything which does not allow light (or other radiations) to pass through it.

OPTICAL FIBRES. Fine glass fibres capable of carrying light.

OPTICS. The study of light.

PENUMBRA. The partial shadow which may surround a total shadow, or umbra.

PHOTON. The smallest particle of light energy.

PLANE SURFACE. A level or flat surface.

POLARIZATION OF LIGHT. Limiting the light vibrations, which are usually going in all directions, to one plane.

PRISM. A transparent construction, usually of glass, which can be used to break visible light down into its separate colours, or as a reflecting medium giving a very pure reflection.

PROTONS. Contained in the centre of all atoms, and carrying a positive electrical charge.

QUARTZ. One of the commonest minerals, known as rock-crystal in its purest form.

QUASAR. Quasi-stars, the reddest light sources in the universe, inexplicably high in energy.

REFLECTION. The bouncing-back of rays of light from a surface on which they have fallen.

REFRACTION. The bending of rays of light which occurs when they pass from one transparent medium to another.

REFRACTIVE INDEX. The exact angle of refraction that will occur when light passes, at a known angle, from one transparent medium into another.

SPEED OF LIGHT. About 300,000 kilometres per second.

SPECTOGRAPH. Instrument which can produce a spectrum on a screen or on a photographic plate.

SPECTROMETER. Instrument for producing and measuring optical spectra.

SPECTROSCOPE. Often a spectrometer joined to a spectrograph, used to observe optical spectra.

SPECTRUM. The result of resolving electro-magnetic radiations in to the separate wavelengths or frequencies of which they are made up.

TOURMALINE. A natural mineral, capable of polarizing light, which is also a gemstone.

TRANSPARENT. Anything which allows light to pass through it.

TRANSVERSE WAVE MOTION. Electric and magnetic vibrations moving at right angles to each other, and at right angles to their direction of travel.

TUNGSTEN. A metal, resistant to chemical action, often used for the filaments in light bulbs.

UMBRA. A sharp shadow—the penumbra is the pale shadow which sometimes surrounds it.

WAVELENGTH. The length between the wavecrests of electro-magnetic vibrations.

XENON. An inert gas (see ARGON) often used in fluorescent lighting tubes.

INDEX

Argon 17
Astronomy 56-58
Astro-physics 56-58
Atoms 15-16, 50, 51

Beams 18
Bending light 27-31
Big Bang Theory 57

Cameras 45
Colour 40-41
        pigment 40
        transmitted 40-41
Concave lenses 35, 36-38
        mirrors 24-25
Convex lenses 35, 39
        mirrors 24
Cosmic rays 8-9, 10
Critical angles 29-30

Diamonds 60
Digital signals 34, 52
Doppler effect 57

Electro-magnetic spectrum 8-12, 56
Electrons 15, 50
Eyes 35-39

Fibre optics 33-34, 52
Fireflies 17
Focal lengths 25-26, 36
Focusing 36-39
Frequencies 9, 51

Gamma rays 8-10
Glass antique 60
        cut 60
        stained 40, 60
Glow worms 17

Holograms 53-55, 59

Infra-red rays 8, 11
Interferometry 55
Irregular reflections 24

Jewellery 60

Kaleidoscopes 24

Lantern fish 17
Lasers 50-52
Lasing mediums 51
Lenses 35-39
Light artificial 17
        natural 11
        speed of 52, 56
        white 11, 40, 41
Long-sight 39
Luminous objects 15-16

Magnifying glasses 47
Microscopes 47
Mirages 34
Mirrors 20-24
Moonlight 16-17

Neutrons 15
Nuclear fission 15, 52
Nuclear fusion 15, 52

Optical fibres 33-34, 52
Optical instruments 39

Painting 59, 61
Penumbra 18
Photons 8, 15, 51
Polarization of light 42-44
Prisms 33, 41-42
Protons 15

Quasars 57-58

Radio telescopes 49, 56
Radio waves 11-12, 31

Rainbows 42
Rays 18, 20
Red shift 57
Reflection 20–26
        laws of 22
        total internal 32–34
Reflector telescopes 47
Refraction 27–32
        laws of 30
Refractor telescopes 47
Refractive index 31, 52
Resonator tubes 51

Shadows 18
Short-sight 38
Spectroscopy 56
Spectrum 9, 11, 41, 56
Spoons, reflections in 25–26

Sunlight 16, 31
Sun sets 31, 61
Swimming pools 29

Telescopes radio 49, 56
        reflector 47
        refractor 47
Tourmaline 42, 44
Total internal reflection 32–34
Transverse wave motion 12
Tungsten 17

Ultra-violet rays 8, 11
Umbra 18

Wavelengths 9, 11, 51

Xenon 51
X-rays 10, 55